THE OFFICIAL GAELIC GAMES ANNUAL 2020

Gill Books
Hume Avenue
Park West
Dublin 12
www.gillbooks.ie

Gill Books is an imprint of M.H. Gill and Co.

© GAA Museum 2019

978 07171 8266 4

Designed by seagulls.net

Printed by L.E.G.O. S.p.A.

The paper used in this book comes from the wood pulp of managed forests. For every tree felled, at least one tree is planted, thereby renewing natural resources.

5 4 3 2 1

For permission to reproduce photographs, the authors and publisher gratefully acknowledge the following:

© Barry Nolan (Wildlife Management Sources): 29T; Courtesy of the GAA Museum: 28BR, 32, 33, 34TL, 35, 39, 40, 55CT, 55BC; © INPHO/Billy Stickland: 36B, 55TCR; © INPHO/Bryan Keane: 6, 25, 54BR, 60; © INPHO/Cathal Noonan: 10L, 11C, 37B, 54C; © INPHO/Donall Farmer: 34TR, 55TC; © INPHO/Gary Carr: 31, 63; © INPHO/James Crombie: 16, 20, 26R, 43, 49TL, 49CL, 49CR, 50B, 51B, 54TR, 54BL, 58, 59; © INPHO/James Meehan: 50T; © INPHO/Ken Sutton: 54BC; © INPHO/Laszlo Geczo: 10R, 16, 42, 55BC; © INPHO/Lorraine O'Sullivan: 11T, 18, 56C; © INPHO/Matthew Browne: 50CL; © INPHO/Morgan Treacy: 55CTL; © INPHO/Oisin Keniry: 8, 9, 45, 61; © INPHO/Ryan Byrne: 7, 29B, 52R, 56B, 57B, 57C, 59BR; © INPHO/Tom Beary: 50CR; © INPHO/Tommy Dickson: 16, 21, 44, 52L, 54CL, 57T; Courtesy of Kyran O'Brien: 37T; Courtesy of Mickey Burke: 26L, 27T, 27BL; © Piaras Ó Mídheach/Sportsfile/Getty Images: 28BL; © Sportsfile: 11B, 19, 24, 27BR, 28, 30B, 30C, 30T, 34BR, 34BL, 36T, 47BL, 47BR, 47TL, 47TR, 51T, 53.

Pp.12–13: GAA Games Development Department

CONTENTS

The Gaelic Athletic Association (GAA) was set up in 1884. It is the biggest sports organisation in Ireland. Every year, thousands of people play hurling, camogie, Gaelic football, handball and rounders around the country and world. There are over 2,200 clubs in Ireland and another 400 clubs in countries like England, America, Canada, China and Australia.

GAA clubs are at the heart of our Gaelic games. They promote the GAA in our local areas and they're where you step out on the pitch for the first time to play with your teammates and friends.

Fill in the details about your own club below and mark where your club is on the map.

MY GAA CLUB IS CALLED: _____

IT IS IN COUNTY: _____

OUR CLUB COLOURS ARE: _____

OUR PITCH IS CALLED: _____

POSITION I PLAY: _____

DRAW YOUR GAA CLUB'S CREST HERE:

MY FAVOURITE GAA SPORT IS: _____

MY FAVOURITE GAA TEAM IS: _____

MY FAVOURITE GAA PLAYER IS: _____

MY COUNTY COLOURS ARE: _____

TREATY COUNTY
PREMIER COUNTY
THE RED HANDS
THE TRIBESMEN
THE CATS
THE ROYALS
DOLMEN COUNTY
DÉISE COUNTY
ORCHARD COUNTY
GLEN COUNTY
OAK LEAF COUNTY
THE LILYWHITES
MARITIME COUNTY
REBEL COUNTY
THE FARNEY
WILD ROSE COUNTY
MODEL COUNTY
BANNER COUNTY
FAITHFUL COUNTY
THE JACKEENS
THE KINGDOM
WEE COUNTY
LAKE COUNTY
MOURNE COUNTY
THE SLASHERS
LAKELAND COUNTY
BREFFNI COUNTY
O'MOORE COUNTY
YEATS COUNTY
O'DONNELL COUNTY
GARDEN COUNTY
THE ROSSIES

CHECK OUT THE ANSWERS ON PAGE 62.

CRAZY COUNTY NICKNAMES

All 32 counties of Ireland have a nickname. Some are very old, dating back to the 13th century. Others come from where they are in Ireland or what their county colours are. You'll hear these being shouted from the stands during matches:

'Hon the Banner!'
'Up the Royals!'

Can you match all the nicknames to the correct county?

BRIAN FENTON

BRIAN FENTON is a powerhouse in midfield for the Dublin senior footballers. This year he claimed his fifth All-Ireland senior football med[al] with the history-making five-in-a-ro[w] Dublin team. He has won all the major honours in Gaelic football and was the 20[ ] All-Star Footballer o[f] the Year.

NAME:
Brian Fenton

AGE:
26

SPORT:
Gaelic football

POSITION:
Midfield

CLUB:
Raheny GAA

COUNTY:
Dublin

ACCOLADES:

5 All-Ireland Senior Football Championships

5 Leinster Senior Football Championships

3 National Football Leagues

3 All-Stars

2018 Footballer of the Year

WHAT'S YOUR FIRST MEMORY OF PLAYING GAA?

I remember training with my local GAA club at the back of the school in Raheny from about 4 or 5. I also remember constantly kicking the ball against the side of my house, pretending I was playing in Croke Park.

WHAT'S YOUR GREATEST GAA ACHIEVEMENT?

Winning the GAA/GPA Footballer of the Year award in 2018.

WHAT'S BEEN THE BIGGEST INFLUENCE ON YOUR GAA CAREER?

My dad. He bought me my first boots and jersey and has stood on the sidelines of almost every game. I play to make him proud. My juvenile managers in Raheny also had a huge influence on my career and taught me everything as a child.

WHAT ADVICE WOULD YOU GIVE TO YOUNGER PLAYERS?

Be obsessed with getting better.

DO YOU HAVE A FAVOURITE PRE-MATCH MEAL?

I always try to focus on meals that will help me perform well on the pitch, so that's always a carbohydrate-heavy meal. For example, some chicken with lots of pasta or rice. Staying well-hydrated is probably the most important thing on match day.

WHO IS YOUR FAVOURITE PLAYER FROM ANOTHER COUNTY?

Lee Keegan is one of the best defenders in the game. His offensive runs can also cut through a team. A fond memory of mine is playing against Colm Cooper in the 2015 All-Ireland final. He is one of the greatest players to ever play.

WHAT'S YOUR FAVOURITE COUNTY GROUND?

Breffni Park in Cavan is a fantastic ground. I also love the Fitzgerald Stadium in Kerry as I've been there plenty of times to watch matches.

WHAT OTHER SPORTS DO YOU ENJOY?

I love watching the Olympics and the excitement of the 4x100m relays in both swimming and athletics. I really enjoy watching basketball in the NBA. Their athleticism is incredible. I also support Manchester United.

COLOURED BOOTS – YES OR NO?

Nothing too crazy. I don't like really bright boots but it depends on the jersey colour too. I prefer wearing black or blue boots.

WHEN DO YOU GET YOUR CHAMPIONSHIP HAIRCUT?

The day before a big championship game.

CATRIONA CASEY

Cork woman **CATRIONA CASEY** has played handball all over the world. She has won many major honours and has been ranked as the number-one player in Ireland and the USA.

WHAT HANDBALL CODES DO YOU PLAY?

I play the 40x20 and 60x30 codes usually. Sometimes I dabble in one-wall and even three-wall (in the US).

WHAT'S YOUR FIRST MEMORY OF PLAYING HANDBALL?

I remember learning to play with my brother and our friends in the local squash court before moving on to the handball court, which seemed so much bigger at the time!

WHAT'S YOUR GREATEST GAA ACHIEVEMENT?

My All-Ireland senior medals are my greatest achievements: four singles and four doubles titles in 40x20, and five singles and six doubles titles in 60x30. Hopefully I can continue to add to this tally! Also, being the number-one ranked player in both Ireland and the US over a number of years.

WHAT'S BEEN THE BIGGEST INFLUENCE ON YOUR GAA CAREER?

I would have to say the biggest influence on my career has been my parents, Dan and Peg, who have driven the length and breadth of the country countless times to support me. I am also very grateful to all the volunteer coaches who helped me get started as a juvenile in my home club and county.

WHICH HANDBALL SHOT IS YOUR FAVOURITE?

Fly-corner kill!

WHAT ADVICE WOULD YOU GIVE TO YOUNGER PLAYERS?

My advice is to spend lots of time on the court on your own, practising your skills with both hands. There are no shortcuts to success, but your hard work really will pay off! Try to get feedback and advice from more experienced players as much as possible and watch the top players whenever you get the chance – you'll learn a lot! Finally, always keep your head up and don't get discouraged in defeat. We usually learn the most from our losses and then come back stronger and even more determined!

DO YOU HAVE A FAVOURITE PRE-MATCH MEAL?

I usually like to have pasta before playing to fuel me for a long match, but it depends on the time of day, really!

WHO IS YOUR FAVOURITE PLAYER FROM ANOTHER COUNTY?

Ducksy Walsh – the proudest Kilkenny man you'd have ever met! He was an outstanding player and person. He excelled in big alley and small alley alike. His records really speak for themselves. I really admired how he was always willing to share insights and encouragement. He was such fun to be around! He is truly missed but will never be forgotten.

WHERE'S YOUR FAVOURITE HANDBALL COURT?

Ballydesmond Handball Club court 1!

WHAT OTHER SPORTS DO YOU ENJOY?

I'm a big sports enthusiast! I played ladies' football up to the age of 20. I also gave camogie a go during my time at Boherbue Comprehensive School. I really enjoy watching all sports, especially tennis. You can play singles and doubles, just like handball!

NAME:
Catriona Casey

AGE:
26

SPORT:
Handball

CLUB:
Ballydesmond

COUNTY:
Cork

ACCOLADES:

4 All-Ireland 40x20 titles

4 All-Ireland 40x20 doubles titles

5 All-Ireland 60x30 titles

6 All-Ireland 60x30 doubles titles

2 Irish 40x20 Nationals titles

1 Irish 1-Wall Nationals title

SUPERSTAR SKILLS

WITH CIAN LYNCH

An All-Ireland winner, league champion, GAA/GPA All-Star and Player of the Year, Limerick's **CIAN LYNCH** knows what it takes to reach the top of his sport. Here's Cian's guide to how you can improve your hurling skills.

GET A GRIP

Your hurley is like an extra hand and should be part of your body. A warrior going into battle would never go without their sword and that is how important the grip on a hurley is. Make it feel like it's part of you.

PRACTICE MAKES PERFECT

Always practise. Spend time practising your good and bad sides so that you will have two good sides and be very hard to mark or predict.

COOL CATCHING

Catching is an important skill in hurling and is key to holding on to primary possession. At training or in matches, try to stop putting the hurley to the ball and start forcing yourself to put your hand to the ball.

PRIME PASSING

When passing the sliotar through hand-passes or striking, always make sure you strike through the ball, rather than a loop. A ball overstruck is better than a ball understruck.

MY SECRET FOR SUCCESS

I try to spend training sessions concentrating on one particular skill. For example, I might dedicate a session to using only my weaker side so I can gain confidence in it.

TRY IT AT HOME

One drill that you can do at home or at training with your teammates is a game of Donkey. Get a group of your friends in a circle and drill the ball at each other. No matter how hard the ball is hit, you are only allowed to catch it with your hand. Train your hand to grab the sliotar.

Always practise and never give up believing. Anything is possible when you put your mind to it. You can achieve anything!

If you want to try out some other drills, turn over to the next page!

HANDBALL: DRIBBLE AND SHOOT

You will need:

This drill is to practise the dribble technique and improve your control over the ball.

1. Split your group into two teams.

2. Set up a line of cones with a target goal area at the end.

3. Each player dribbles the ball with their hands between the cones along the floor. When you reach the end, shoot and score a goal.

4. Pick up the ball, run back and hand it to the next player.

5. The first team to score 10 goals wins.

PRACTICE MAKES

Practice really does make perfect. All the best GAA players will tell you that they practise their skills and techniques whenever they have a free minute. Why not try these drills at home with your friends to improve your skills? Be careful, don't try these indoors!

FOOTBALL: BOUNCE AND TURN

You will need:

This drill is to practise the bounce technique.

1. Set up four cones in a square about five metres apart.

2. Position one player, ball in hand, at each cone.

3. Each player runs to another cone at random, bouncing the ball.

4. Try using your left hand to bounce the ball when turning to the right around a cone, and your right hand when turning to the left.

ROUNDERS: STRIKE

You will need:

This drill is to practise ball-handling, carrying and striking skills.

1. Divide into pairs, with one player standing at each cone.

2. Player B feeds the ball to Player A at waist height.

3. Player A bats the ball with a hurley to Player B, who catches it.

4. Swap after 10 rounds, and make sure to switch between over- and under-arm throwing.

PERFECT

HURLING/CAMOGIE: SIGNAL AND TURN

You will need:

This drill is to practise the dribble technique. It challenges you to change direction on a signal.

1. Using the cones, mark out a distance of 10 metres.

2. Each player lines up at each cone on one side with their hurley and sliotar. One player uses the whistle to signal.

3. On the signal, each player dribbles towards their opposite cone.

4. When the player signals with their whistle again, each player quickly changes direction and dribbles back to their cone.

5. The player with the whistle should vary the point at which they signal to keep the players on their toes.

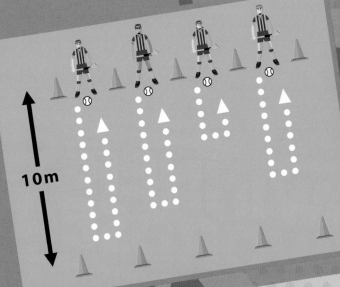

10m

It takes a lot of hard work and effort to play for your county. Can you find the 15 things you need to become the best player you can?

JERSEY	RESPECT	FOOTBALL
HELMET	REFEREE	HANDBALL
TEAMWORK	WHISTLE	GOAL
SLIOTAR	COACH	POINT
HURLEY	DEDICATION	PRACTISE

```
B  U  R  I  F  T  L  X  T  D  T  E  Y  R  K
A  U  F  J  U  X  U  L  E  B  S  I  E  E  R
M  N  Q  Q  S  U  J  D  A  I  H  V  L  S  O
O  V  P  W  Q  I  I  D  T  B  K  B  R  P  W
G  C  Q  A  Q  C  N  C  U  R  D  K  U  E  M
C  R  P  S  A  H  A  W  E  N  M  N  H  C  A
R  C  E  T  G  R  E  A  R  Q  T  L  A  T  E
R  T  I  F  P  S  L  I  O  T  A  R  K  H  T
G  O  E  Q  E  T  P  W  Y  E  S  R  E  J  Y
N  O  P  M  N  R  H  L  L  A  B  T  O  O  F
C  D  A  I  L  I  E  S  P  U  M  R  W  R  A
U  L  O  L  S  E  G  E  L  A  I  D  M  J  I
N  P  Q  T  F  X  H  I  M  A  T  J  Z  Z  Y
B  F  L  C  O  A  C  H  A  P  R  A  S  B  U
P  E  O  J  W  Q  Z  M  J  Q  M  R  X  C  K
```

WINNER'S WORDSEARCH

CHECK OUT THE ANSWERS ON PAGE 62.

SIDELINE SUDOKU

Use the clues below to fill in the missing squares and finish off the sudoku.

Remember you can only use each symbol once in every line and mini-grid.

CHECK OUT THE ANSWERS ON PAGE 62.

KIT BAG CHAOS

Oh no! These county players have gotten their gear mixed up on the way to their big matches! Can you match the four players to the correct jersey, shorts and socks they're meant to wear on the day?

CATHAL McSHANE

LEE CHIN

CONOR COX

BRENDAN MAHER

A

B

C

D

A

B

C

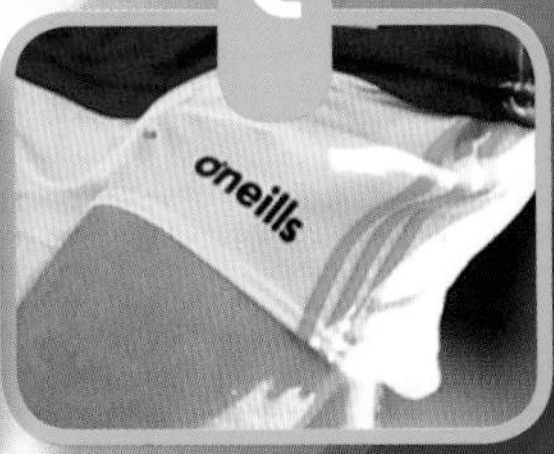

D

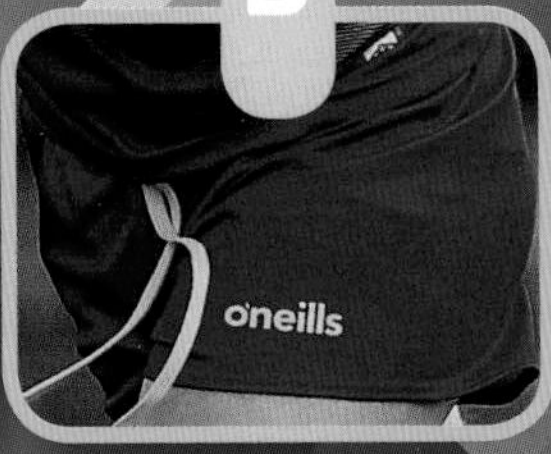

A

B

C

D

MY GEAR IS ...

JERSEY SHORTS SOCKS

MY GEAR IS ...

JERSEY SHORTS SOCKS

MY GEAR IS ...

JERSEY SHORTS SOCKS

MY GEAR IS ...

JERSEY SHORTS SOCKS

CHECK OUT THE ANSWERS ON PAGE 63.

Sometimes matches can be won or lost with a single shot. It takes a very skilled player to be able to poc the sliotar or kick the ball over the bar and score the winning point on the day!

Can you work out who scores the winning point here?

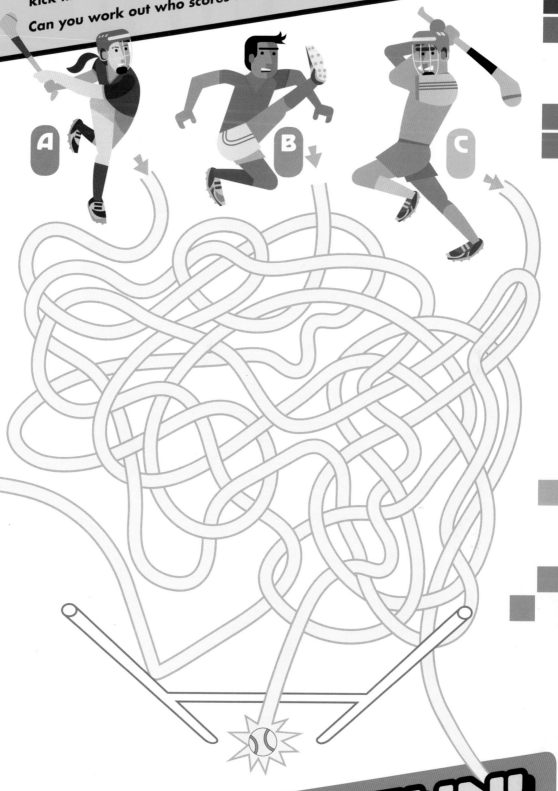

CHECK OUT THE ANSWERS ON PAGE 63.

POC FADA FUN!

EVE O'BRIEN

EVE O'BRIEN shines on the Dublin senior camogie team as a full-back. She knows a thing or two about on-pitch rivalries! Eve also worked in Croke Park as a tour guide for the **GAA Museum** in summer 2018!

WHAT'S YOUR FIRST MEMORY OF PLAYING GAA?

I remember playing mini-leagues when I was five during the summer. I had a jersey that went down to my knees and my helmet was too big!

WHAT'S YOUR GREATEST GAA ACHIEVEMENT?

My greatest achievement is representing Dublin camogie in our first All-Ireland championship semi-final in 27 years in 2017. I'll never forget the feeling of running out onto the pitch that day.

WHO IS YOUR FAVOURITE PLAYER FROM ANOTHER COUNTY AND WHY?

Siobhán Flannery from Offaly. She's the hardest player I've ever marked – pure class.

WHAT'S YOUR FAVOURITE COUNTY GROUND?

Innovate Wexford Park.

WHAT'S BEEN THE BIGGEST INFLUENCE ON YOUR GAA CAREER?

My parents and my brother. My parents coached my team when I was growing up, and now they come to all my matches, supporting and encouraging me always. My brother taught me how to strike the ball.

WHAT ADVICE WOULD YOU GIVE TO YOUNGER PLAYERS?

There's no such thing as perfection. Every time you take to the field you will make mistakes. Mistakes are the best way to learn and improve. Don't be too hard on yourself and enjoy it!

DO YOU HAVE A FAVOURITE PRE-MATCH MEAL?

The night before a big match I have a steak with veg and sweet potatoes.

WHAT OTHER SPORTS DO YOU ENJOY?

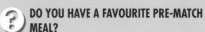

I used to play basketball, which I loved. I like watching rugby, boxing and water polo.

COLOURED BOOTS – YES OR NO?

Yes! They make you look faster.

NAME:
Eve O'Brien

AGE:
26

SPORT:
Camogie

CLUB:
CLG Na Fianna

COUNTY:
Dublin

POSITION I PLAY:
Full-back

ACCOLADES:

1 National League Division 4

1 Dublin League Division 1

Purcell Cup

MEET THE PLAYERS
RICHIE HOGAN

RICHIE HOGAN is a star of the Kilkenny senior hurling team, one of the most successful teams in the country. He's won everything, including All-Ireland medals, Leinster titles, National Hurling League medals and All-Star awards!

NAME:
Richie Hogan

AGE:
31

SPORT:
Hurling

CLUB:
Danesfort GAA Club

COUNTY:
Kilkenny

POSITION I PLAY:
Centre-forward

ACCOLADES:

7 All-Ireland Senior Hurling Championships

8 Leinster Senior Hurling Championships

4 National Hurling Leagues

4 All-Stars

2014 Player of the Year

WHAT'S YOUR FIRST MEMORY OF PLAYING GAA?

My first playing memory is playing with my brother and friends at John Locke's GAA club, which my father was playing in during the early '90s. We would hurl on the sidelines for hours while he was playing in a league or championship game for his club.

WHAT'S YOUR GREATEST GAA ACHIEVEMENT?

Winning any All-Ireland is a great achievement. I have been lucky to win it seven times and every one of those has been an incredible achievement by the team.

WHO IS YOUR FAVOURITE PLAYER FROM ANOTHER COUNTY AND WHY?

My favourite player from another county is Ken McGrath from Waterford. I was lucky to play against him on many occasions. He was very versatile and played in multiple positions in a great Waterford team in the '00s.

WHAT'S YOUR FAVOURITE COUNTY GROUND?

My favourite county ground is Nowlan Park in Kilkenny. I worked there for four summers as a student and I saw the care that Mick O'Neill and Timmy Grogan put into the pitch and the stadium. It is the perfect capacity, easily accessed and the pitch is always in incredible condition.

WHAT'S BEEN THE BIGGEST INFLUENCE ON YOUR GAA CAREER?

My family are huge GAA people in different ways. Whether it is tradition, advice, lifts to training, pre-match meals, support or encouragement, everything comes from some part of my extended family at different times.

WHAT ADVICE WOULD YOU GIVE TO YOUNGER PLAYERS?

Keep practising and trying all the time, no matter how good or bad you may feel you might be now. So many players improve later in their careers, when others have lost interest. At underage level, players are different sizes, ages and strengths, but once you get to 22–23 years old, everyone evens out and the work you have done will then start to pay off.

DO YOU HAVE A FAVOURITE PRE-MATCH MEAL?

I vary my pre-match meals all the time. As long as I have enough protein and carbohydrates on the plate with as little fats as possible, then I'm happy. Chicken, sweet potato and vegetables, or chicken pasta with a tomato-based sauce are probably my most common pre-game meals.

WHAT OTHER SPORTS DO YOU ENJOY?

I played handball and soccer until I was 19. Then for me it was time to concentrate on hurling at the highest level. Now, I enjoy watching all sports on TV and attending events whenever I get the time.

COLOURED BOOTS – YES OR NO?

No!

WHEN DO YOU GET YOUR CHAMPIONSHIP HAIRCUT?

I get my hair cut every four weeks or so. For me I usually need to get a championship beard trim. If it gets too long, my mother insists I tidy myself up for the cameras!

TOP-SECRET
BANISTEOIRÍ TACTICS

Club and county managers – or banisteoirí – are often seen standing on the sidelines during matches, shouting out advice and encouraging their players. They come up with ways for their team to perform better on the day.

This GAA manager keeps his tactics a secret by writing them in code! Can you decipher the message below and figure out how the team will play? All you need to do is use the code to unlock the message!

I think _____
will win the **2020 All-Ireland
hurling championship** because:

_____

_____

I think _____
will win the **2020 All-Ireland Gaelic
football championship** because:

_____

_____

I think _____
will win the **2020 All-Ireland ladies'
Gaelic football championship**

because:

_____

_____

I think _____
will win the **2020 All-Ireland
camogie championship** because:

_____

_____

WHO'S GOING TO WIN?

What teams do you think will be
champions in 2020 and why?
Draw and colour in their county flags.

Don't forget to look back at the
end of the 2020 championships to
see if your predictions were right!

MEET THE PLAYERS
SINÉAD BURKE

All-Star defender **SINÉAD BURKE** made her senior inter-county debut for Galway in 2007. This year, she played a key role in helping her county reach the All-Ireland senior ladies' football final for the first time in 14 years.

WHAT IS YOUR FIRST MEMORY OF PLAYING GAA?

Playing under-10s with the boys' team in Oughterard with only four other girls!

WHAT IS YOUR GREATEST ACHIEVEMENT?

My greatest achievement would have to be receiving an All-Star in 2018.

DO YOU HAVE A FAVOURITE PRE-MATCH MEAL?

No favourites but we always seem to get chicken and pasta!

WHO IS YOUR FAVOURITE PLAYER FROM ANOTHER COUNTY?

Sinéad Goldrick from Dublin. She plays in a similar position to me. I always enjoy watching her play and the way she can influence a game.

WHAT IS YOUR FAVOURITE COUNTY GROUND?

Pearse Stadium, Galway.

WHO HAS BEEN THE BIGGEST INFLUENCE ON YOUR CAREER?

The biggest influence on my sporting career has definitely been my dad. I used to watch him play football every week from a young age and he used to always drop me off at and pick me up from training. He's been my number-one supporter and has always been there for me.

WHAT OTHER SPORTS DO YOU ENJOY?

I used to play basketball and would love to get back to playing it again.

WHAT ADVICE DO YOU HAVE FOR YOUNG PLAYERS?

It's hard to beat a person who never gives up!

ACCOLADES:

1 All-Ireland Senior Ladies' Gaelic Football Championship

9 Connacht titles

1 National League Division 2

1 All-Star

Lynch Cup

NAME:
Sinéad Burke

AGE: 29

SPORT:
Gaelic football

POSITION: Back

CLUB:
Ballyboden St Enda's, Dublin (formerly Killannin, Co. Galway)

COUNTY:
Galway

MY GAA LIFE
WITH MICKEY BURKE

Meath dual star MICKEY 'THE HONEYBADGER' BURKE is famous off the pitch for his tattoos and rock-star hair, but he's also well-known on the pitch for his serious skills, strength and commitment to the games he loves.

FIRSTS + FAVOURITES

DEBUTS

I first played senior hurling for Longwood when I was 15. I was called to the Meath hurlers when I was 16 and I made my debut for the Meath footballers in 2004, when I was 18. Seán Boylan was my manager — he was a god to me.

MY FIRST GAA MEMORY

Going to Meath games with my mother and father — they gave me a great love of GAA.

MY FAVOURITE GAA MOMENT

Celebrating with my parents after winning the Meath intermediate football club championship with Longwood — it was our first in 80 years!

MY GAA HEROES

Darren Fay and Trevor Giles — I loved the way they played. Outside Meath, I looked up to Kieran McGeeney.

DREAMS DO COME TRUE

Everything starts with a dream. We had a huge wall out the back of our family pub. I would kick a ball against it morning, noon and night, dreaming of playing for Meath. I was shocked to be called up for Meath. No one from Longwood had played football for Meath before, so it was out of the blue and I was young.

FOOTBALL + HURLING

PLAYING DUAL CODES

I love both codes. I come from hurling territory in south Co. Meath, so I grew up with a hurl in my hand. Playing both codes can be tough. Sometimes you play two games in two days! I feel like both codes complement each other well.

CLUB AND COUNTY

I love my club, Longwood GAA, and playing with my best friends, cousins and family! We are still all playing together since under-10s, when my dad trained us. Playing for Meath is a huge honour. As a kid, I dreamed of wearing the Meath jersey. Thankfully, with hard work, it came true!

TIPS FOR SUCCESS

Always do your best. Whether things are going good or bad for you, keep running and keep trying hard. Football-wise, practise with both feet kicking off a wall.

FAMILY + FRIENDSHIPS

THE BIGGEST INFLUENCES

My mother and father brought me to training and Meath games. My dad coached me underage and played for Meath years ago!

SUPPORT AND LOYALTY

No matter what happens, your friends and family will be there for you.

FRIENDS FOR LIFE

I love the friendships you make through the GAA. I roomed with Bonner Maher from Tipperary when we were on the Irish hurling squad. We are still good mates.

FAMILY COMES FIRST

I help my dad feed the cattle and the sheep. We are very busy around calving and lambing season. We have goats as well — they take minding! It's great to be active and out in the fresh air. It's physical work but it keeps you strong and fit.

FITNESS + FOOD

TRAIN, TRAIN, TRAIN

I love training and always have. My training consists of pitch sessions, gym work, my own running and ball work. Recently, I've taken up Bikram yoga.

PRE-MATCH PREP

I've no major superstitions. I like to be prepared. I lay out all my gear the night before to make sure I don't forget anything. I don't eat much the day of a game as I would be nervous. Nerves aren't bad, though. It is my body telling me I'm ready! I would eat foods with slow-releasing energy the day before a match: things like porridge, potatoes, sweet potatoes, sourdough bread, fresh fruit and vegetables and plenty of water!

EAT YOUR VEGETABLES!

I love healthy eating. Eating well is so important for sport. It helps you perform better and recover quicker. Eat your vegetables, as your mother would say!

FALLS + KNOCKS

INJURIES

I've broken my leg and hurt ligaments in my knee. I was out for 10 months. It's important to stay positive if you get injured. I had a positive mindset and was very driven about getting back playing. I did everything the doctor told me 110%. There is always light at the end of the tunnel.

KEEP YOUR HEAD UP

Keep positive and keep doing your best — your team needs you! In loads of games, I haven't played well but that doesn't mean that I don't try. I always did my best. The ball might not have bounced my way, but I kept running and kept positive.

FASHION

MY WOOLLY HAT

My green-and-gold woolly hat was knitted by my mother! I wear it to remind me of her before games. I like to think of people who are close to me before matches.

BE YOURSELF

I have always been my own man. I have had long hair, tattoos and coloured boots, but it's important not to let that affect you. I was just being myself, but I always trained hard. I never got arrogant or cocky. It is so important to be yourself, but don't let it affect your playing. Stay grounded. I'm still trying to get better and improve.

FUN FACT

I played under-17 and under-19 badminton for Leinster. Longwood has a good badminton club and my mother was a great player!

CRAZY ABOUT CROKE PARK

Croke Park is the headquarters of the GAA. It is one of the biggest stadiums in Europe and has played host to many iconic moments in Irish sporting history. Every year, supporters flock to Croke Park to watch Gaelic football, hurling and camogie matches. It's very exciting to see the stadium full of people, proudly dressed in their county colours, supporting their teams!

The pitch at Croke Park measures 144m x 86m. The total grass area of Croke Park is 14,000m². That's almost twice the size of a standard soccer or rugby pitch!

EAGLE EYES

Sometimes, seagulls swoop down into the stadium and grab food from people or steal it before it can be properly recycled. Pigeons can also eat newly laid grass seed and nest under the stadium roof. On match days, a specially trained team of hawks is brought in to keep these pesky birds away! Sometimes, pretend hawks that look like kites are used too.

The GAA Museum made history in Croke Park by setting a Guinness World Record for Largest Hurling Lesson on 30 September 2018. To celebrate the museum's 20th birthday, 1,772 children from clubs across Ireland took part in a half-hour training session. It was an amazing sight to see them on the pitch under the floodlights with their club mentors, representing all four provinces of Ireland. It was a tough record to achieve, and everyone had to stick to the lesson plans and follow the drills, but the young GAA players achieved the record on the night!

RECORD BREAKERS!

During the winter, the pitch is mowed at least twice a week. During the summer, the pitch can be mowed up to ten times a week! This is to keep the height of the grass at 30mm, which is the perfect length for playing both football and hurling.

In busy cities where there are not many green spaces, it's hard for insects to find places to live and hibernate. Birds also struggle to find safe places to build their nests. Near the Cusack Stand entrance at Croke Park, you will find specially made bird boxes. These have been used by blue tits to nest and rear their young for the last few years. Croke Park is also home to the Bug Bee & Bee. It's made from natural materials and provides shelter and safe nesting areas for lots of bugs and insects! Over 80 tonnes of compost waste is collected from Croke Park each year. This is taken to the Croke Park turf farm. Here, it's used to help grow turf for the pitch. Beehives have been installed at the farm to give busy bees somewhere safe to live and feed.

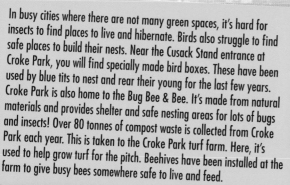

SNUG BUGS AND BUSY BEES

Almost 90 fixtures are played in Croke Park every year, as well as concerts, charity games and events. Last year, Croke Park was used for 584 hours of activity!

PLAY THE CÚL WAY!

Kellogg's GAA Cúl Camps inspire the Gaelic footballers, hurlers and camogie players of the future. Cúl Camps are held during the summer holidays in all 32 counties of Ireland. They are an action-packed and fun-filled week of activities for 6–13 year olds. More than 150,000 children took part in a Kellogg's GAA Cúl Camp this year. Were you one of them?

The capacity of Croke Park is 82,300 people. The largest attendance ever recorded at Croke Park is 90,556. It was for Offaly v Down in the 1961 All-Ireland football final!

There's a famous stand at Croke Park called Dineen Hill 16. It's named in honour of Frank Dineen, who first bought the site where Croke Park stands today. It was originally called Hill 60, named after the Battle of Hill 60 in Gallipoli, where Irish men fought in World War I. Many people think that Hill 16 was built using rubble from O'Connell Street after the 1916 Rising, but this isn't true. The Hill was already completed in time for the 1915 All-Ireland finals. Ask your parents about this — they might still think this myth is true. Now you can tell them the real story!

HURLING HERITAGE

Hurling is an ancient sport that's been played for thousands of years, passed on from older people to younger people. In Ireland, we've always known how important it is, and now the whole world knows too. In 2018, hurling and camogie were added to UNESCO's Lists of Intangible Cultural Heritage. This means that our great games will be carefully protected for thousands of years to come!

You can find out more historic facts on page 40.

DINEEN HILL 16

BEHIND THE SCENES AT CROKE PARK

There's a lot of people who work hard behind the scenes at Croke Park to make sure big match days and other events run smoothly. ELAINE CASEY is Croke Park's Event Controller. She looks after thousands of visitors to the stadium and makes sure everyone has a good time.

Name: Elaine Casey

Job: Croke Park Event Controller

Club: St. Finian's (camogie) and Fingal Ravens (football)

County: Dublin

Slua - Today's Attendance
FULL HOUSE

TELL US ABOUT THE WORK YOU DO AT CROKE PARK?

My role on match day is to make sure everything goes safely and smoothly. I organise all the staff, including voluntary stewards, security, gardaí, customer care, the accessibility team and the medical team.

There are lots of preparations before any event happens at Croke Park. I make sure that information about the upcoming fixtures goes out to everyone involved behind the scenes. This includes details about who's playing, throw-in times and how many people are expected to attend. All of this helps us to have a safe and well-organised event.

WHERE CAN WE FIND YOU DURING A BIG MATCH DAY?

On a match day, I sit in the Control Room. It's under the big screen on Dineen Hill 16! We keep an eye on everything going on across the stadium and use CCTV, phones and radios to keep in touch. There can be up to 400 people with radios on match day. We even have a pair of binoculars to see everything easily!

WHAT DO YOU ENJOY MOST ABOUT YOUR JOB?

My job is very different every day. I manage all the big GAA games but I also organise the GAA Go Games and Cumann na mBunscol days, where children from all around the country come to play in Croke Park. Everyone is so excited to play on the famous turf!

I also help organise the concerts. These are hard work but really enjoyable. I've helped organise concerts for Coldplay, Taylor Swift, Spice Girls and Westlife!

Looking after VIP visits to the stadium is also a fun part of my job, such as welcoming the Duke and Duchess of Sussex in 2018, and the King and Queen of Sweden this year.

WHAT'S YOUR FAVOURITE THING ABOUT WORKING IN CROKE PARK?

I really enjoy the atmosphere and excitement that comes with an important match or exciting event. It's great to know that you are there on the days, playing a part in making history.

WHAT'S YOUR FAVOURITE CROKE PARK MEMORY?

It's really hard to pick just one but a stand-out memory was Limerick winning the Liam MacCarthy Cup in 2018. The utter joy in the stadium was incredible!

WHAT DO YOU LIKE TO DO OUTSIDE WORK?

I don't stray too far from GAA! I love to play camogie with my local club, St Finian's.

CAN YOU REVEAL ANY BEHIND-THE-SCENES SECRETS ABOUT CROKE PARK?

We have over 360 volunteers who give up their time to welcome and look after our 1.2 million spectators every year!

Croke Park match-day numbers:

Number of turnstiles: *99*

Number of ticket scanners: *119*

Number of CCTV cameras: *222*

Number of staff at an All-Ireland final: *3,290*

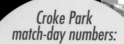

This photo was taken during the exciting Leinster hurling final played between Wexford and Kilkenny in Croke Park on 30 June 2019. It was a historic match as Wexford beat their rivals Kilkenny to become Leinster champions for the first time in 15 years!

Take a close look at the images below and see if you can spot the 8 differences.

A

B

HAWK-EYES!

CHECK OUT THE ANSWERS ON PAGE 63.

THE GAAzette

4 SEPTEMBER 1939

World War II begins as Kilkenny win the thunder and lightning final

Kilkenny: 2-7 | Cork: 3-3

Jimmy Kelly scored a dramatic last-minute point to help Kilkenny beat their Rebel rivals Cork in an action-packed All-Ireland hurling final yesterday. 39,302 supporters gathered to watch the match in Croke Park, which was played in terrible weather conditions as rain poured down, thunder crashed and lightning flashed in the Dublin venue. The game, now called the 'Thunder and Lightning Final', took place on a day that history will never forget – when World War II broke out in Europe.

15 SEPTEMBER 1947

Big win in the Big Apple for the Breffni County

Cavan: 2-11 | Kerry: 2-7

Kerry and Cavan's travels to America ended in a four-point win for the Ulster men in yesterday's All-Ireland football final in New York. This game was a very special one because it is the only All-Ireland football final to have been played outside Ireland. The historic match was played in the Polo Grounds, which is usually used for baseball games. A crowd of over 36,000 supporters attended the final and thousands of people listened to it on the radio back home in Ireland.

20 SEPTEMBER 1982

Darby's wonder goal ends Kerry's four-in-a-row roll

Offaly: 1-15 | Kerry 0-17

A late goal from Offaly hero Séamus Darby in yesterday's All-Ireland football final ended Kerry's dreams of winning five titles in a row. With just two minutes left in the match, the Kingdom's Drive for Five was alive as they led by two points at Croke Park. In any match, it's important to keep playing until the end and this is exactly what Offaly did. With the game almost over, super-sub® Darby struck the ball high into Kerry goalkeeper Charlie Nelligan's net to score a goal and win the Sam Maguire Cup for the Faithful County.

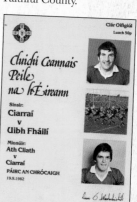

For the third year in a row, the All-Ireland hurling final has ended in a draw, as Kilkenny and Tipperary couldn't be separated at Croke Park yesterday. The teams will meet again on 27 September. When Clare met Cork in the 2013 final, the teams also drew. The year before, after 70

8 SEPTEMBER 2014

2014 hurling champions still not known as final ends in draw for third year in a row

Kilkenny: 3-22 | Tipperary: 1-28

minutes of hurling, the final between Kilkenny and Galway also ended all square. Before 2012, the last All-Ireland hurling final to finish in a draw was in 1959. Uachtarán Cumann Lúthcleas Gael Liam O'Neill will have the special record of being GAA President for six All-Ireland hurling finals during his three years in office – something that has never happened before!

THIS JUST IN!

Imagine you're a newspaper reporter writing about a final in 2020. The final could feature your school, club or county team.

Write your own newspaper article about the final. Make sure to have a catchy headline and tell the story of the game. Include details about the teams, venue, score, who played well, what the weather was like and how many people were at the match!

THE GAAZETTE

Send us your news report and be in with a chance to win a family pass for a Croke Park stadium tour and access to the GAA Museum!

WIN

To find out how to enter and for terms and conditions, go to page 63.

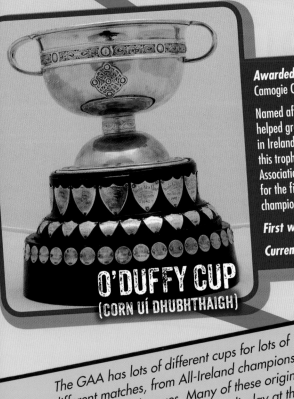

O'DUFFY CUP
(CORN UÍ DHUBHTHAIGH)

Awarded to: All-Ireland Senior Camogie Champions

Named after Seán O'Duffy, who helped grow camogie's popularity in Ireland. Seán presented this trophy to the Camogie Association of Ireland in 1932 for the first All-Ireland championship.

First winners: Dublin

Current winners: Galway

Awarded to: All-Ireland Senior Hurling Champions

Named after Liam MacCarthy, who was a former president of the London GAA county board. The cup has been presented every year since 1923.

First winners: Limerick

Current winners: Tipperary

LIAM MacCARTHY CUP
(CORN MHIC CÁRTHAIGH)

The GAA has lots of different cups for lots of different matches, from All-Ireland championships to regional club leagues. Many of these original iconic cups can be seen today on display at the **GAA Museum**.

ICONIC CUPS

Awarded to: All-Ireland Senior Ladies' Gaelic Football Champions

Named after Brendan Martin, who helped set up the Ladies' Gaelic Football Association (LGFA). Brendan donated this cup to the LGFA in 1974 for their first All-Ireland championship.

First winners: Tipperary

Current winners: Dublin

BRENDAN MARTIN CUP
(CORN BHREANDÁIN UÍ MHÁIRTÍN)

SAM MAGUIRE CUP
(CORN MHIG UIDHIR)

The Sam Maguire Cup is awarded to the All-Ireland Senior Football champions. It is made of solid silver and based on the design of the Ardagh Chalice. It weighs 12 pounds and is 16 inches high. It is named after Sam Maguire, a Cork man who lived in London and was very active in the GAA there. Kildare were the first team to win the cup in 1928. They haven't won it since! Stephen Cluxton from Dublin has lifted the cup more than anyone else on All-Ireland final day. Dublin are the current All-Ireland senior football champions. A replica cup is now presented on final day. The original can be seen in the GAA Museum!

To find out how to enter and for terms and conditions, go to page 63.

WIN

Send us your cup design and you could be in with a chance of winning a Croke Park goodie bag. We have 5 to give away!

Páirc an Chrócaigh
CROKE PARK

Why don't you have a go at designing your own trophy? Winning a trophy is a big deal, so make sure it's bright and colourful!

Don't forget to write down what your cup would be awarded for. It could be for something on or off the pitch and can be at any level – a prize for your local club, an All-Ireland, or even a world championship!

THIS CUP IS AWARDED TO: _____

DESIGN YOUR OWN CUP

MY CAMOGIE LIFE
WITH ANNA GEARY

ANNA GEARY is a camogie player from Cork. She has won 4 All-Ireland medals and 6 All-Stars! She's as skilled on the pitch as she is on the dancefloor!

WHEN DID YOU FIRST START PLAYING?

I started playing when I was 6 years old. Milford, a small village in Cork, is my home club. I've been so lucky to play with so many different teams throughout the years. I wasn't very good when I was young, but I played to make friends and enjoyed being part of a team. As I got older, I got more confident and I gradually improved.

WHAT'S YOUR FIRST MEMORY OF PLAYING?

I remember being at our local GAA pitch, huddled in a circle with all my teammates. Our coach was reminding us of the basics of camogie: how to hold the hurley, lock your hands and pull hard on the ball. We were so small. Our jersey sleeves were coming down past our elbows!

WHAT POSITION DID YOU PLAY?

I played midfield when I was younger. I had the speed and loved the freedom of being able to roam. As I got older, I moved towards the half-back line. I have played in every position throughout my camogie career, except goalkeeper. I don't know how they do it! Number 7, wing-back, will always be my favourite position.

WHAT'S YOUR GREATEST ACHIEVEMENT?

Captaining Cork to All-Ireland glory in 2014 was a dream come true. I made a promise to myself that if I ever got the chance to raise the cup, I would run up the steps of the Hogan Stand to the podium. I lost my speech notes on the way up, but the words came to me anyway!

Winning our first senior club All-Ireland title with Milford was such a pinch-me moment. Standing on the hallowed turf of Croke Park with girls I had grown up with was so special. Looking at the sea of supporters in the stand is a memory I'll never forget.

WHO IS YOUR FAVOURITE PLAYER FROM ANOTHER COUNTY?

I was always a huge fan of Offaly legend Brian Whelahan. I loved his consistency, leadership, composure and humility on the field. He always did the right thing for the team – selfless and self-confident at the same time. As a fellow left half-back, I aspired to play like him. I met him at the GPA Awards in 2005. It was one of the rare times in my life that I've been speechless!

National Fitness Day 2018 27th September

WHAT'S YOUR FAVOURITE GROUND YOU PLAYED IN DURING YOUR CAREER?

I loved playing in Croke Park, because as a camogie player that meant you were playing in an All-Ireland final. There is something special about the atmosphere of Semple Stadium, Thurles. We played Wexford in the 2012 National League final. The Cork support was like our 16th player that day. You could feel the energy pouring out from the stands. It was brilliant!

ARE THERE OTHER SPORTS OR ACTIVITIES YOU ENJOY?

I love watching most sports and have dabbled in a few others. Athletics was one. And despite cross-country running being a part of my teenage years, I wasn't designed for long distances. I'm not a bad sprinter, though! Even in high heels!

Last year, being on *Dancing with the Stars* reminded me of how much I love dancing. I'd love to take up some form of dance. It's a great workout and so much fun! Sport brings people together, no matter what the sport is.

WHAT WAS THE BIGGEST INFLUENCE ON YOUR CAREER?

My parents were the biggest influence on my career. I'm so grateful to them for being my taxi service for about 15 years, taking me to training and matches.

When I was younger, my mam was a positive and reassuring force for me. She encouraged me to keep trying, no matter how many times I failed. My dad nurtured my competitive spirit. He helped me to understand that you need to have commitment and discipline in order to excel. He taught me that working hard and leadership are vital attributes to have as a sportsperson.

WHAT ADVICE WOULD YOU GIVE YOUNGER PLAYERS?

'Teamwork makes the dream work.' You have to work together to succeed.

Don't be afraid to make mistakes. Failure is not a weakness. It's a strength, because it shows you were brave enough to try!

Lastly, sport isn't about winning or medals and trophies. It's about the memories and friends you make and the fun and experiences you have. Make every second count!

GAA players and supporters wear their club and county jerseys with pride. On match days, Ireland's towns and villages are full of people wearing their team colours.

HAVE YOUR OWN JERSEY SPECIALLY MADE FOR YOU!

WINNING JERSEYS

WIN

Design your own GAA jersey – one that you would be proud to wear on the pitch. Don't forget to include your lucky number on the back!

Send us your design and you could be in with a chance of having it made specially for you!

To find out how to enter and for terms and conditions, go to page 63.

Here's Offaly hero Séamus Darby's jersey that he wore in the famous 1982 All-Ireland football final, when he stopped Kerry's dream of winning five in a row. He scored a goal with just two minutes to spare. Do you think it looks different to the jerseys players wear today?

There are lots of cool jerseys and artefacts on display at the **GAA Museum**. Read more about the **GAA Museum** on page 40!

WELCOME TO THE

GAA MUSEUM
CROKE PARK

A trip to Croke Park wouldn't be complete without a visit to the **GAA Museum**. The GAA Museum is like no other museum in the world. It celebrates the history of Ireland's national games and is home to lots of interesting artefacts and exhibitions!

Come and see these Awesome Artefacts at the **GAA Museum**!

FIND YOUR CLUB!

You'll also find the Club Wall outside the GAA Museum. Here you can see all the crests of GAA clubs around the country and world. When you come to visit, make sure to have a look at the Club Wall to find your club crest!

falla na gclub
CELEBRATING 125

MEET CLUASÓG

As the GAA Museum's mascot and captain of Cluasóg's Club of Junior Explorers, Cluasóg does special tours and has created a special fun trail in the museum for you to explore.

VINTAGE RADIOS

Long before TV, the Internet and Wi-Fi, people followed GAA matches by listening to them on the radio!

GREAT GLOVES

Croke Park has hosted many other events such as rugby, soccer, American football and boxing matches. On 19 July 1972, one of the world's most famous boxers, **Muhammad Ali**, fought Al 'Blue' Lewis in Croke Park. You can see his shorts and one of his boxing gloves on display in the GAA Museum.

You'll find out all about GAA heroes throughout the years in the GAA Museum Hall of Fame. Look at these boots from the 1960s. They belonged to Down All-Ireland-winning Gaelic footballer **Seán O'Neill**. They are very different from the boots that modern players wear today!

HALL OF FAME

Lory Meagher Medal Collection

National Hurling League 1932

Inter-Provincial (Railway Cup) 1926

Leinster Senior Hurling Championship 1926 1936

On loan fro

Ki Cha

MARVELLOUS MEDALS

Jack Lynch All-Ireland Medal Collection

Donated by

All-Ireland Senior Hurling Championship
1941 1942 1943 1944 1946

All-Ireland Senior Football Champion
1945

The GAA Museum has lots of medal collections on display from some of the greatest legends of the games, like Armagh Gaelic footballer **Oisín McConville**, Cork dual star and former taoiseach **Jack Lynch**, Dublin camogie player **Kathleen Mills**, Cork dual star **Mary O'Connor** and Kilkenny handballer **Michael 'Ducksy' Walsh**.

The winning All-Ireland captains also receive their very own mini Sam Maguire or Liam MacCarthy cup.

OLD-SCHOOL GEAR

If you were a hurler in 1888, you would've played with a sliotar and hurley like this!

CAMOGIE COSTUME

If you played camogie in 1904, this is what you would have worn! Imagine trying to run around a pitch dressed like this!

MICHAEL CUSACK

GAA MUSEUM

Michael Cusack is a very important name in the GAA. On 1 November 1884, he and six others met at Hayes Hotel in Thurles, Co. Tipperary. There, they set up the GAA to promote the sports around the country. Without him, we might not be playing GAA today!

AOIFE NÍ CHAISIDE

AOIFE NÍ CHAISIDE is a camóg from Co. Derry. In March, Aoife made history with her clubmates from Robert Emmets GAC, Slaughtneil, when they won their third All-Ireland senior club camogie title in a row.

WHAT'S YOUR FIRST MEMORY OF PLAYING GAA?

Playing on my front lawn at home with my six siblings, sometimes shooting against Mammy in goals!

WHAT'S YOUR GREATEST GAA ACHIEVEMENT?

Winning three All-Ireland senior club titles in a row and being captain of the first ever winning team.

WHO IS YOUR FAVOURITE PLAYER FROM ANOTHER COUNTY AND WHY?

Rena Buckley from Cork. What an athlete and a lovely person! I aspire to be as committed to camogie as she is to her sports.

WHAT'S YOUR FAVOURITE COUNTY GROUND?

Donaghmore Ashbourne, Co. Meath.

WHAT'S BEEN THE BIGGEST INFLUENCE ON YOUR GAA CAREER?

My mammy and daddy, Thomas and Anne Marie. They started my love for the game. When I was growing up, my Slaughtneil clubmate Claire Doherty inspired me as a camogie player. In more recent years, Dominic 'Woody' McKinley has willingly shared his knowledge.

WHAT ADVICE WOULD YOU GIVE TO YOUNGER PLAYERS?

I would advise young players to take their hurls with them on holidays. We always did and had great fun pocking about on the beaches. I even had my hurl at the top of Carrauntoohil mountain with me!

DO YOU HAVE A FAVOURITE PRE-MATCH MEAL?

The morning of a match, Mammy makes us porridge and my uncle Christopher supplies the various toppings, usually fresh fruit and nuts.

WHAT OTHER SPORTS DO YOU ENJOY?

I enjoy participating in Pilates classes. Also, basketball and table tennis for fun.

COLOURED BOOTS – YES OR NO?

Personally, no.

NAME:
Aoife Ní Chaiside

AGE: 25

SPORT:
Camogie

CLUB:
Robert Emmets GAC, Slaughtneil

COUNTY:
Derry

POSITION I PLAY:
Centre half-back

ACCOLADES:

3 All-Ireland Senior Club Camogie Championships

3 Ulster Senior Club Camogie Championships

2018/19 Club Camogie Team of the Year

ROBBIE McCARTHY

Handball champion **ROBBIE McCARTHY** is known nationally and internationally for his skills on the court. He's even known as 'Buzzsaw' McCarthy in America for his strength and determination!

WHAT HANDBALL CODES DO YOU PLAY?
60x30, 40x20 and 1-wall.

WHAT'S YOUR FIRST MEMORY OF PLAYING HANDBALL?
Running through the door of the old ball alley in Mullingar. I couldn't wait to get onto the court.

WHAT'S YOUR GREATEST GAA ACHIEVEMENT?
I must say the one win I will never forget is the 2017 60x30 All-Ireland final, the year we played for the Ducksy Walsh Cup. When I was a young lad, I watched Ducksy play and I played him in tournaments as I got older. It's an absolute honour to have my name on his cup – that moment will stick with me forever.

WHAT'S BEEN THE BIGGEST INFLUENCE ON YOUR GAA CAREER?
My dad, Robbie Snr. He pulls all the strings and has been at 99% of my games. He is always there for me, no matter what, win or lose.

WHICH HANDBALL SHOT IS YOUR FAVOURITE?
The paddle kill!

WHAT ADVICE WOULD YOU GIVE TO YOUNGER PLAYERS?
Never give up and keep trying. I think once you are playing a sport you enjoy and keep training, you will get there. Learn from your losses, stay humble with your wins and, above all, make it count.

DO YOU HAVE A FAVOURITE PRE-MATCH MEAL?
Of course! On game day I have a routine, but nothing beats a cup of tea with a few rich tea biscuits.

WHO IS YOUR FAVOURITE PLAYER FROM ANOTHER COUNTY?
Ducksy Walsh and Tom Sheridan would be two of my sporting heroes. Both are legends of the 60x30 game and displayed nothing but class and skill in their games. They always had great banter with the crowds and opponents.

WHERE'S YOUR FAVOURITE HANDBALL COURT?
Mullingar!

WHAT OTHER SPORTS DO YOU ENJOY?
I enjoy going to the gym but I played a lot of football and hurling growing up.

WHEN DO YOU GET YOUR CHAMPIONSHIP HAIRCUT?
I get my hair cut on the Thursday before game day. It's just routine now. There was no particular reason at the start but I just kept it going then.

ACCOLADES:
2 World 40x20 doubles titles
7 All-Ireland 60x30 titles
4 All-Ireland 40x20 titles
3 Irish 40x20 national titles
2 Irish 1-wall national titles

NAME:
Robbie McCarthy

AGE:
32

SPORT:
Handball

CLUB:
Mullingar

COUNTY:
Westmeath

Did you know that GAA isn't just played in Ireland? There are GAA clubs all over the world so that Irish people who live and work abroad can play the games they love. There are over 400 clubs overseas – from Antrim to Australia, Cork to Canada, Dublin to Dubai and Sligo to Shanghai.

Some of these clubs have very cool names and crests!

 MOSCOW SHAMROCKS, MOSCOW, RUSSIA

 VIKING GAELS, SCANDINAVIA

 HELSINKI HARPS, FINLAND

ROCKAWAY ROVERS, NEW YORK, US

 ARABIAN CELTS, BAHRAIN AND EASTERN SAUDI ARABIA

ORANG ÉIRE, MALAYSIA

CELTIC COWBOYS, AUSTIN, TEXAS, US

Celtic Cowboys GAA Club is based in Texas, US. The club was set up in 2004. They compete at state level, against clubs in Dallas, Houston and San Antonio, and at national level with other American teams. Last year, they won the ladies' junior B and men's intermediate football titles. They even hosted their first Cúl Camp this summer!

GAA AROUND THE WORLD

LONDON AND NEW YORK

London and New York do not appear on a map of Ireland, but these cities have close links to Ireland and are very important to the GAA. London and New York have their own teams that take part in GAA competitions. In 2019, football and hurling teams from London played in the National Hurling League, National Gaelic Football League, Connacht Gaelic Football Championship and the Christy Ring Cup. A team from New York participated in the Connacht Gaelic Football Championship, too.

RENAULT GAA WORLD GAMES

The Renault World Games is a competition that celebrates the global growth of Gaelic games and gives players a chance to win world titles in Gaelic football, ladies' Gaelic football, hurling and camogie. The first GAA World Games took place in Abu Dhabi in 2015.

The 2019 games were staged in Ireland and the eight finals took place in Croke Park in August. There were four finals for Irish-born players and another four finals for non-native players. The tournament brought together over 1,300 participants from 97 teams, representing clubs from a wide range of areas across Europe, as well as New York, South Africa, Argentina, Canada, Britain, Australasia, India, Asia and the Middle East.

The winners were:

RENAULT GAA WORLD GAMES HURLING
Native champions: New York GAA
Irish champions: Middle East GAA

RENAULT GAA WORLD GAMES CAMOGIE
Native champions: Twin City Robert Emmets, Minneapolis/St Paul, Minnesota, USA
Irish champions: Australasia GAA

RENAULT GAA WORLD GAMES LADIES' FOOTBALL
Native champions: New York Liberty
Irish champions: Australasia GAA

RENAULT GAA WORLD GAMES FOOTBALL
Native champions: New York Freedom
Irish champions: Middle East GAA

THE DRIVE FOR FIVE

Winning five All-Ireland senior championship titles in a row is something that had never been achieved by any Gaelic football or hurling team in the history of the GAA ... until 2019!

The Wexford senior footballers were the first team to ever win four All-Ireland titles in a row – they were champions from 1915 to 1918. In 1919 their winning streak came to an end when they were beaten by Dublin in the 1919 Leinster semi-final.

From 1929 to 1932, Kerry were the top team. The Kingdom's first Drive for Five ended in 1933, when Cavan defeated them in the All-Ireland senior football semi-final.

A four in a row was also achieved by the Cork senior hurlers between 1941 and 1944, but they lost to Tipperary in the 1945 Munster semi-final.

When Kerry senior footballers won four All-Ireland titles in a row between 1978 and 1981, their Drive for Five was alive once again. They made it all the way to the final in 1982 but lost out by just 1 point to Offaly.

From 2006 to 2009, Kilkenny hurlers claimed the Liam MacCarthy Cup for four years in a row. The Cats got all the way to the All-Ireland final in 2010 but were beaten by Tipperary.

Only one senior team has been successful in their drive for five.

FAMOUS FIVE

The Dublin senior footballers won four All-Ireland titles in a row from 2015 to 2018. They beat Kerry in the final in 2015, Mayo in the finals in 2016 and 2017, and Tyrone in the final in 2018.

On 1 September 2019, Dublin came up against their old rivals Kerry in the All-Ireland senior football final. It was an exciting and close match, and it finished in a draw. The two teams had to play again. The replay took place on Saturday, 14 September. When the final whistle blew, Jim Gavin's boys in blue came out champions and made history by becoming the first senior team in Gaelic football or hurling to win five in a row!

DUBLIN'S DRIVE FOR FIVE 2015–2019

YEAR	TEAM AND SCORE	TEAM AND SCORE
2015	Dublin: 0-12	Kerry: 0-09
2016	Dublin: 2-09	Mayo: 0-15
2016 replay	Dublin: 1-15	Mayo: 1-14
2017	Dublin: 1-17	Mayo: 1-16
2018	Dublin: 2-17	Tyrone 1-14
2019	Dublin: 1-16	Kerry: 1-16
2019 replay	Dublin: 1-18	Kerry: 0-15

MY FOOTBALLING FAMILY
WITH RYAN McHUGH

Donegal footballer RYAN McHUGH talks about what it's like to be part of one of Ireland's most famous footballing families.

TEAM McHUGH

MARTIN McHUGH (RYAN'S DAD)
All-Ireland senior football winner 1992
Player of the Year 1992
All-Star Award 1983, 1992

JAMES McHUGH (RYAN'S UNCLE)
All-Ireland senior football winner 1992
All-Star Award 1992

MARK McHUGH (RYAN'S BROTHER)
All-Ireland senior football winner 2012
All-Star Award 2012

RYAN McHUGH
Young Player of the Year 2014
All-Star Award 2016, 2018

HAVE YOU ALWAYS BEEN A BIG GAELIC FOOTBALL FAMILY?

Ever since I can remember, Gaelic football has always been a huge part of my family. My father played and managed teams as I was growing up, so I would always go along with him to games. Myself, my brother Mark and sister Rachel would always be outside playing football – kick-passing and hand-passing to each other.

DID YOU GROW UP LISTENING TO STORIES ABOUT THE GAA?

When I was growing up my Granny McHugh would always have the 1992 All-Ireland football final on in her house. It was the first time Donegal won Sam Maguire and my father and my uncle James were on the team. I was always hearing stories about them and seeing them play as I grew up. I think people think having a father or uncle who were great footballers can put pressure on you. I didn't think like this at all. I tried to use them to my advantage and gain as much advice and experience from them and use that to make myself a better player.

IS YOUR WHOLE FAMILY INVOLVED IN THE GAA?

All my family members are involved in the GAA in some way. My father played for Kilcar and Donegal. He also managed Cavan and Kilcar later in his career. My mother is our number-one supporter in everything we do. She's never missed a match that any of us have played in. My brother Mark plays for Donegal and Kilcar. My sister Rachel played football for Kilcar also. Rachel is like mum, she would not miss matches of ours and loves going to support us, which is great.

WHY IS THE GAA SO SPECIAL TO YOUR FAMILY?

My family loves the GAA. When we sit down, there's not much else talked about in the McHugh household other than GAA! It's the main topic at breakfast, dinner and teatime. Most of our closest friends have been made through the GAA. People know when they come into the McHugh household, they'll be talking about it. I wouldn't have it any other way.

WHAT'S IT LIKE IN YOUR HOUSE IN THE LEAD-UP TO A BIG MATCH?

In the lead-up to a match, we try to be calm. I feel if you're more calm and collected, you'll perform better. It's all we'll be talking about in the house, so it's hard sometimes not to be excited. My parents will give advice on what to do, so I try to take on board what they say as they're more experienced than me and have been through it all before.

After the matches, it will depend on the result. If we win the match, everyone will be in great form and happy. Unfortunately if we lose, everyone will be disappointed.

YOUR FAMILY HAS AN AMAZING RECORD OF WINNING ALL-STARS – YOU MUST BE VERY PROUD!

Yes, it's something my family is extremely proud of. We are extremely fortunate that we had the chance of getting an All-Star.

My father won his first All-Star in 1983. It was a huge moment for him personally and the family. In 1992, he won his second All-Star. The same year, my uncle James won his All-Star and Donegal won the All-Ireland, with the two of them playing brilliantly throughout the year. My father also won Player of the Year that year. That would have been a huge moment for the McHugh family!

In 2012, my brother Mark won an All-Star and Donegal won the All-Ireland that year. This was another huge moment for the family and was my first experience of being at the All-Stars. In 2014, I won Young Player of the Year, which was a great achievement. Then in 2016 and 2018, I won my All-Stars. I was extremely happy and proud of myself and I feel my family were too. We had great nights in Dublin at the All-Star events, each one as good as the one before it. I just hope we can have many more nights at the All-Stars!

WHAT HAS THE GAA GIVEN TO YOUR FAMILY?

The short answer would be everything. I could not imagine my life without the GAA. The GAA has given my family and myself the opportunity to play at the highest level in the sport we love, and we will be forever grateful.

BORN TO PLAY GAA

WITH MATTHEW O'HANLON

Wexford senior hurling captain MATTHEW O'HANLON was born to play GAA. Here, the St James's clubman shares what it's like to lead his county out in Croke Park, the top tips from Davy Fitz, and advice on how to live and play well.

NAME:
Matthew O'Hanlon

AGE:
28

SPORT:
Hurling

CLUB:
St James's GAA Club

COUNTY:
Wexford

POSITION I PLAY:
Centre-back

DRESSING ROOM SECRETS

? WHAT DO YOU DO BEFORE A MATCH?

I don't have any match-day rituals. I'm not very superstitious. I like listening to music before games, to zone out of the distractions around me and focus on my own job. I just put on whatever music I'm into at the time of the game.

? HOW DO YOU STAY ON TOP DURING A GAME?

At half-time, we try to take in water, isotonic sports drinks and orange segments to refuel as much as possible.

? WHO'S THE BIGGEST JOKER ON THE TEAM?

There are a few jokers on the team. The biggest ones are probably Éanna Martin or Lee Chin!

? WHO TAKES THE LONGEST TO DO HIS HAIR?

Diarmuid O'Keefe!

WEXFORD'S WINNING WAYS

Croke Park was a sea of purple and gold on 30 June when Wexford beat Kilkenny with a score of 1-23 to 23 points to win their first senior Leinster hurling title in 15 years!

FAMILY FOOTSTEPS

I've been playing GAA for as long as I can remember. I come from a GAA family. My grandfather Mick O'Hanlon played hurling for Wexford in the 1950s (alongside the legendary Rackards), winning Leinster, League and All-Ireland titles. My dad, Luke, has been involved in GAA all his life, playing Gaelic football and hurling for Horeswood and Wexford. He would have been my biggest influence growing up.

TOP TIPS FROM DAVY FITZ

One of the things Davy always encourages us to do is train to improve. In every drill and every session we do, we focus on what we are trying to improve, whether that's shooting, first touch or tackling.

LEADING THE PURPLE AND GOLD

It's a huge honour for me to be chosen as captain of the Wexford senior hurlers, along with Lee Chin. It's special for me as I'm the only one from my club and family to ever do it. It's a great feeling running out onto the pitch and hearing the roar of the supporters. It gives you a huge boost and gets the adrenaline going!

CAPTAIN'S WINNING ADVICE

TRAIN YOUR MIND AND YOUR BODY

I research the players I'm likely to mark, looking for their strengths and weaknesses, how they play and try to score, so I know what to expect. I'm always trying to learn from those around me, listening to what my coaches and selectors want me to work on, such as first touch, pick-ups, high balls, passing, shooting and tackling.

GET OUT, GET ACTIVE, GET BETTER

I love the outdoors, so I try to get outside and keep active as much as possible. Most days I'll be out pocking around with friends, down at the beach, in the gym, or going for a walk. You're always in a better mood after you exercise!

EATING WELL IS A GAME CHANGER

Nutrition is a huge part of a GAA player's life. Eating healthily has a big impact on how you perform on the pitch. It's important to vary the types of food you're eating and make sure to get enough of all food groups into your diet.

BE A GREAT MATE

In your team or school, it's always important to keep an eye out for your friends around you. If you notice someone who isn't in good form, be sure to check in with them to make sure everything is okay. A simple conversation to make someone feel included can go a long way. In our team, we try to share our problems. A problem shared is a problem halved, as the saying goes!

TALK, TALK, TALK

If you're feeling worried about something in school, or if you're annoyed with yourself about how you played in a match, don't get upset or feel bad. Talk it out with a friend or family member. Being able to share any problem you have is important. Bottling it up isn't a good way to overcome it.

TO BE THE BEST, GET PLENTY OF REST

It's important to rest and recover to get the best out of yourself on and off the pitch. Sleep is a massive part of this. Try to get at least 8 hours every night.

THE BIG GAA QUIZ

1

What year was the All-Ireland senior football final played in New York?

2

What team won the 2019 Munster senior hurling championship?

3

What county does Conor McManus play for?

4

Name the stands in Croke Park.

5

Which county team wears a black and red jersey?

6

Name the cup awarded to the All-Ireland senior ladies' football champions.

7

Name the band that regularly plays on match day in Croke Park.

8

What's the name of the stadium in Thurles, Co. Tipperary?

9

What club won the 2019 All-Ireland senior club camogie championship?

10

Name the first county to win the Sam Maguire Cup.

11

What county has the nickname the Faithful County?

12

What province is Pearse Stadium in?

13

What year was the GAA set up?

14

What is the capacity of Croke Park?

15

What county won the 2019 Ulster senior football championship?

16

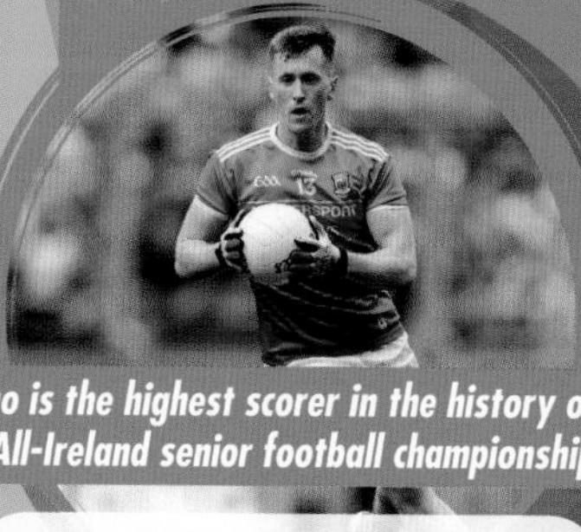

Who is the highest scorer in the history of the All-Ireland senior football championship?

17

What city is Nowlan Park in?

18

Who are the 2019 Joe McDonagh Cup champions?

19

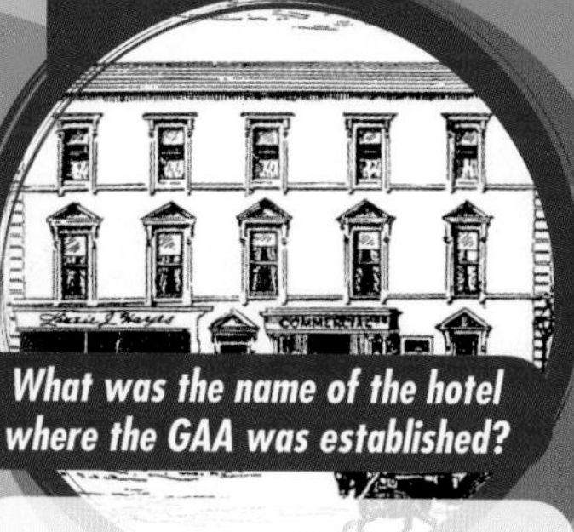

What was the name of the hotel where the GAA was established?

20

Name the Gaelic games commentator from County Clare.

CHECK OUT THE ANSWERS ON PAGE 63.

HIGHLIGHTS OF THE YEAR

INDIVIDUAL PERFORMANCE OF THE YEAR (FOOTBALL)

Jack McCaffrey was Dublin's star man in the first All-Ireland senior football final, which ended in a draw. His performance had everything: lightning-fast pace, great defending, top support play and excellent scoring. A footballer that always enjoys what he does, Jack racked up 1-3 in the drawn match. His first-half goal was an awesome effort and a very important score for his team.

COMEBACK OF THE YEAR

Things weren't looking good for the Cavan ladies when they were 11 points down during their TG4 All-Ireland senior championship round 1, group 1 game against Armagh, but thanks to a super second-half performance and goals from Lauren McVeety, Aisling Sheridan and Aisling Maguire, they came back to win by one point: 3-18 to 6-08. This makes it the highest-scoring one-point game in the history of ladies' championship football!

DEBUT OF THE YEAR

Waterford man Darren Mulhearne made his senior inter-county debut this summer at the age of 46, when he got called up to play in goals for the Déise county's senior footballers in their Munster quarter-final clash against Clare. Proof that your dreams can come true at any age!

TEAM SPIRIT OF THE YEAR

After winning the Joe McDonagh Cup on 30 June, the Laois hurlers clashed with Dublin in the All-Ireland preliminary quarter-final on 7 July. Despite being the underdogs, the Laois men hurled heroically and beat Dublin with a final score of 1-22 to 0-23. This qualified them for their first All-Ireland quarter-final since 1979!

SUPPORTERS OF THE YEAR

When Leitrim senior footballers made it to the Allianz football league division 4 final against Derry on 30 March, it seemed like the entire county came to cheer them on. The Leitrim supporters brought great colour, noise and excitement with them to Croke Park. Leitrim people living around the world even travelled back for the match. It was the first time Leitrim appeared in Croke Park in 13 years — only their fifth ever time to play in GAA HQ! Although the Leitrim men lost the final, they still gained promotion to a higher league division for the first time since 1990!

TURNAROUND OF THE YEAR

The Electric Ireland All-Ireland minor football final between Cork and Galway at Croke Park on 1 September was every bit as exciting as the senior game that followed it! Galway's Niall Cunningham scored a goal late into stoppage time to put his side 3 points in front. It looked like the Tom Markham Cup was going west but Cork never gave up and, 30 seconds later, their inspirational captain Conor Corbett scored a great goal for the Rebels, to force the game to extra time. Cork went on to win (Cork 3-20; Galway 3-14) and became All-Ireland minor football champions for the first time since 2000. It shows how important it is to play until the final whistle!

POINT OF THE YEAR

Clare minor hurler Seán Ronan showed unbelievable technique in the closing stages of the Electric Ireland Munster hurling minor championship semi-final on 16 June. He managed to get around four Cork defenders, control the sliotar and sail it over the bar from an impossible angle. Ronan's score was crucial to Clare. It levelled the game for them and they went on to win by just one point. Clare 0-18; Cork 2-11.

RECORD BREAKERS

On 9 June 2019, Dublin captain Stephen Cluxton made history by becoming the first player in either Gaelic football or hurling to make 100 appearances in the championship, when Dublin and Kildare met in the Leinster senior football championship!

On 13 July, Mayo sharp shooter Cillian O'Connor set a new record when he became the highest scorer in the history of the All-Ireland senior football championship, overtaking Kerry legend Colm 'Gooch' Cooper's record of 23 goals and 283 points.

GOAL OF THE YEAR

When Mayo footballers played against their neighbours Galway in the All-Ireland senior football championship round 4 qualifier game on 6 July, Mayo star James Carr scored two goals in three minutes to help his team beat their Connacht rivals (Mayo 2-13; Galway 1-13). Carr's second goal was extra special and skilful. He powered through the Galway defence and rocketed the ball into the back of the net! The sensational strike has been watched online by millions of people around the world!

LEADER OF THE YEAR

Tipperary hurling captain Séamus Callanan led by example throughout the year. A real goal-getter, the star forward from Drom-Inch hit the net in each of Tipperary's eight championship matches. He blitzed the Kilkenny backs in the All-Ireland final, scoring 1-2 as he guided his side to the Liam MacCarthy Cup. Callanan now holds the record of being Tipperary's highest goal scorer of all time!

INDIVIDUAL PERFORMANCE OF THE YEAR (HURLING)

Cork hurling sensation Patrick 'Hoggie' Horgan scored a phenomenal 3-10 for the Rebels against Kilkenny in the All-Ireland senior hurling championship quarter-final on 14 July in Croke Park. The Glen Rovers clubman scored an incredible 7-62 in the 2019 senior hurling championship!

2019 ALL-IRELAND HURLING CHAMPIONS

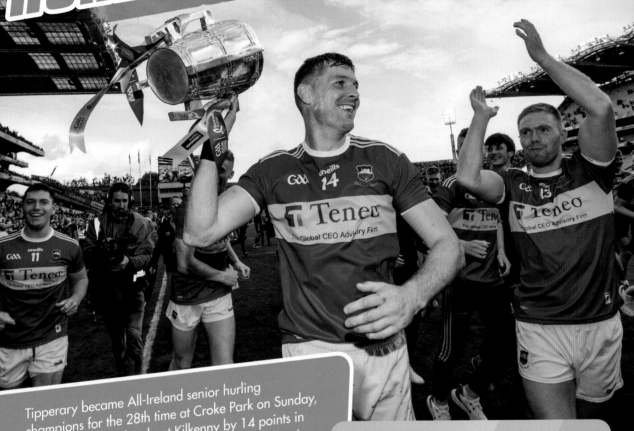

Tipperary became All-Ireland senior hurling champions for the 28th time at Croke Park on Sunday, 18 August, when they beat Kilkenny by 14 points in the final, which was played in showery conditions in front of 82,300 supporters.

Managed by Liam Sheedy, the Tipperary men bounced back after their Munster final loss to Limerick, to beat Laois and Wexford on the way to their Croke Park clash against the Cats. The first-half of the final was very close, with Tipperary leading by 1 point at the break, 1-09 to 0-11. In the second-half, the Munster men were outstanding and scored a whopping 2-16 to record a famous win over their big rivals.

This was the Premier County's third All-Ireland hurling title this decade. They also won the Liam MacCarthy Cup in 2010 and 2016.

TIPPERARY

2019 ALL-IRELAND SENIOR HURLING CHAMPIONS

18 AUGUST 2019

CROKE PARK

TIPPERARY: 3-25

KILKENNY: 0-20

2019 Munster senior hurling champions: **Limerick**

2019 Leinster senior hurling champions: **Wexford**

DID YOU KNOW?

Thurles (Tipperary) were the winners of the first ever All-Ireland hurling championship in 1887.

DUBLIN

2019 ALL-IRELAND SENIOR GAELIC FOOTBALL CHAMPIONS

CROKE PARK

1 SEPTEMBER 2019

DUBLIN: 1-16

KERRY: 1-16

14 SEPTEMBER 2019 (REPLAY)

DUBLIN: 1-18

KERRY: 0-15

When Dublin and Kerry met in the All-Ireland senior Gaelic football final on Sunday, 1 September, the exciting and action-packed game finished level. The two teams met again for the replay on Saturday, 14 September, and 82,300 spectators watched as another dramatic match took place in a sun-soaked Croke Park.

At the end of the first-half, the score was 10 points each, meaning that even after over 100 minutes of football, the sides still couldn't be separated! Less than one minute into the second-half, Dublin's Eoin Murchan scored a wonder goal to give Dublin the lead. Kerry battled back with some excellent points but Jim Gavin's side powered on to win a historic five in a row and lift the Sam Maguire for the seventh time this decade.

2019 ALL-IRELAND GAELIC FOOTBALL CHAMPIONS

DID YOU KNOW?
Commercials (Limerick) were the winners of the first ever All-Ireland football championship in 1887.

2019 Ulster senior football champions: **Donegal**

2019 Munster senior football champions: **Kerry**

2019 Leinster senior football champions: **Dublin**

2019 Connacht senior football champions: **Roscommon**

Galway were crowned the Liberty Insurance All-Ireland senior camogie champions at Croke Park on Sunday, 8 September. A record crowd of 24,730 watched the exciting and high-scoring game.

Galway's goals came in the 18th, 26th and 28th minutes, leaving them 6 points up at the break. Kilkenny worked hard in the second-half and managed to close the gap to 2 points, but the Galway girls showed great skill and determination to hold on to their lead and win the O'Duffy Cup.

This was Galway's third ever All-Ireland senior camogie title. They also won in 1996 and 2013.

2019 brought double delight for the Tribeswomen as they also claimed the Littlewoods Ireland camogie league division 1 title!

GALWAY

2019 ALL-IRELAND SENIOR CAMOGIE CHAMPIONS

8 SEPTEMBER 2019

CROKE PARK

GALWAY: 3-14

KILKENNY: 0-17

2019 ALL-IRELAND CAMOGIE CHAMPIONS

All-Ireland intermediate camogie champions: **Westmeath** (Westmeath 1-11; Galway 1-09)

All-Ireland junior camogie champions: **Kerry** (Kerry 0-11; Limerick 0-08)

2019 ALL-IRELAND LADIES' FOOTBALL CHAMPIONS

DUBLIN

2019 ALL-IRELAND SENIOR LADIES' GAELIC FOOTBALL CHAMPIONS

15 SEPTEMBER 2019

CROKE PARK

DUBLIN: 2-03

GALWAY 0-04

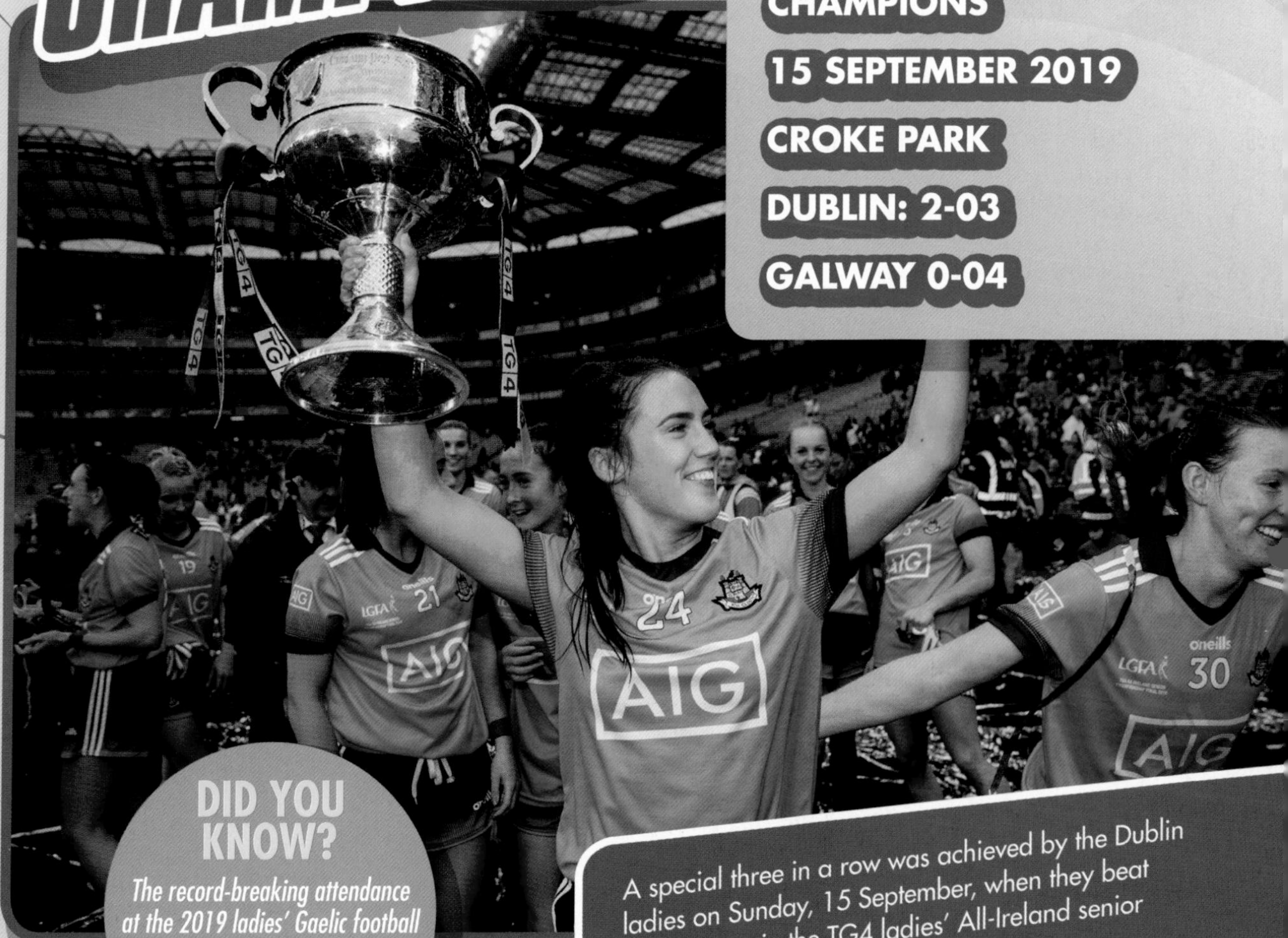

DID YOU KNOW?

The record-breaking attendance at the 2019 ladies' Gaelic football finals in Croke Park makes it one of the largest women's sports events in Europe!

All-Ireland intermediate ladies' Gaelic football champions: **Tipperary** (Tipperary 2-16; Meath 1-14)

All-Ireland junior ladies' Gaelic football champions: **Louth** (Louth 3-13; Fermanagh 2-06)

A special three in a row was achieved by the Dublin ladies on Sunday, 15 September, when they beat Galway to win the TG4 ladies' All-Ireland senior football final at Croke Park.

The rain, which fell throughout the game, made conditions difficult for both sides and scores were hard to get, with a Dublin goal and a Galway point the only scores on the board at half-time.

During the half-time break, presenter Marty Morrissey announced the terrific news to the crowd that the attendance was 56,114 – a record-breaking figure for ladies' Gaelic football!

In the second-half, another goal from the girls in blue kept them well ahead for the rest of match, winning them the Brendan Martin Cup once again.

EXTRA TIME
THE ANSWERS

5 CRAZY COUNTY NICKNAMES

NICKNAME	COUNTY
Treaty County	Limerick
Premier County	Tipperary
The Red Hands	Tyrone
The Tribesmen	Galway
The Cats	Kilkenny
The Royals	Meath
Dolmen County	Carlow
Déise County	Waterford
Orchard County	Armagh
Glen County	Antrim
Oak Leaf County	Derry
The Lilywhites	Kildare
Maritime County	Mayo
Rebel County	Cork
The Farney	Monaghan
Wild Rose County	Leitrim
Model County	Wexford
Banner County	Clare
Faithful County	Offaly
The Jackeens	Dublin
The Kingdom	Kerry
Wee County	Louth
Lake County	Westmeath
Mourne County	Down
The Slashers	Longford
Lakeland County	Fermanagh
Breffni County	Cavan
O'Moore County	Laois
Yeats County	Sligo
O'Donnell County	Donegal
Garden County	Wicklow
The Rossies	Roscommon

14 WINNER'S WORDSEARCH

```
B U R I F T L X T D T E Y R K
A U F J U X U L E B S I E R R
M N Q Q S U J D A I H V L E O
O V P W Q I I D T B K B R P W
G C Q A Q C N C U R D K U E M
C R P S A H A W E N M N H C A
R C E T G R E A R Q T L A T E
R T I F P S L I O T A R K H T
G O E Q E T P W Y E S R E J Y
N O P M N R H L L A B T O O F
C D A I L I E S P U M R W R A
U L O L S E G E L A I D M J I
N P Q T F X H I M A T J Z Z Y
B F L C O A C H A P R A S B U
P E O J W Q Z M J Q M R X C K
```

15 SIDELINE SUDOKU